New Issues Press

Western Michigan University 1903 West Michigan Ave.   Kalamazoo, MI 49008   269-387-8185 Fax 269-387-2562   www.wmich.edu/newissues

Editor:

Herbert Scott

New Issues Press Announces the Publication of
Little Low Heaven by Anthony Butts
Release Date: April, 2003

Little Low Heaven is Anthony Butts' second volume of poetry. His first, *Fifth Season,* was described by Sherod Santos as ". . . a triumph not only of his art, but of his own indomitable spirit as well." Born and raised in inner-city Detroit. Anthony Butts attended a school for the blind and the retarded through the eighth grade before "testing" into a regular high school. The details of his life are particularly devastating. That he survived is miracle enough.

Now, with wisdom and insight Anthony Butts has authored a second book of poems that is brilliant in its brutal yet empathetic vision of America. *Little Low Heaven* makes its bows to loneliness and yearning, to the necessity

Advisory Editors:

J.D. Dolan

Stuart Dybek

Nancy Eimers

Jaimy Gordon

Mark Halliday

Arnold Johnston

Richard Karrovas

William Olsen

Herbert Scott

S0-AXM-833

LITTLE LOW HEAVEN

POEMS

BY ANTHONY BUTTS

A Green Rose Selection
Publication Date: Spring 2003

$14.00 Trade Paper   59 Pages   ISBN:1-930974-26-4

"We must have faith in what's not given," writes Anthony Butts in *Little Low Heaven*, his extraordinary new volume of poetry. Seldom is a second book by a young poet so philosophically ambitious, and yet so vulnerable in its intimacy. Beginning with a journey through the streets of Detroit, where "The act of wanting offers / only the hope of movement," and ending with an apocalyptic vision in which survivors lower a gangplank onto "a new continent / that will come to own us no more / nor haunt us any less," *Little Low Heaven* describes a world of isolation and beauty, art and prophecy, loss and yearning. In his tender yet terrible reading of the human condition, Anthony Butts has become a poet of pain and sorrow and, finally, of the barest budding of hope.

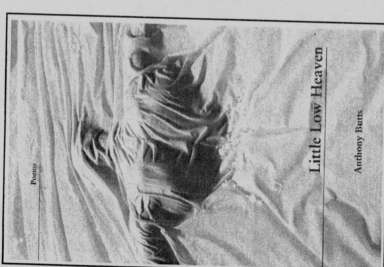

Poems

Little Low Heaven

Anthony Butts

Praise for Fifth Season:

"*Fifth Season* is, I think, both proof and triumph of Chi

Poem to be Hummed

I am standing before a gathering of those
whose eyes are a gentle sea barely visible, all of us viewing
something near the poetry that isn't us,
nor the poet as he was then, nor even some fellow rowing,
keenly aware of his small presence:
a void so familiar we dare not fear it
or ask why we don't recall it in other moments.

Where do visions go? To the same
sanctuary as jazz artists at the completion
of a set—that magical green room we've only dreamt of?
Are we not something other than what we are?
The slender librarian in a sheer flowered dress,

Most of us know the green room
was never meant for us but for the mythological
jazz man with all his faults, unable to switch off
whatever it is within us that we could never
switch on, our emotions like acute angles—
more a fear of consumption by mouths
than the opposing pull of what we see before us:
that we seek out the myths that we believe in,
an endless space having enveloped us long ago.

demons and angels are equally acknowledged, equally real, and equally allotted their place in the poems. That any first book can manage such a feat is, in itself, remarkable; that Anthony Butts has done it in a style and a music all his own is a triumph not only of his art, but of his own indomitable spirit as well. In another time, we might have called this 'grace.' —Sherod Santos

Photo by Matt Bulvony

Anthony Butts is also the author of *Fifth Season*. His work appears on *Our Souls Have Grown Deep Like the Rivers*: *Black Poets Read Their Work*; in *Giant Steps: The New Generation of African American Writers*; and in *American Poetry: The Next Generation*. A Detroit native, he is a graduate of Wayne State University and the University of Missouri-Columbia, and a member of the creative writing faculty at Carnegie Mellon University in Pittsburgh, Pennsylvania.

NEW ISSUES POETRY & PROSE

WESTERN MICHIGAN UNIVERSITY, 1903 W. MICHIGAN AVE., KALAMAZOO, MI 49008-5331

Bookstore Orders:

Small Press Distribution, Inc (SPD)
(800) 869-7553
www.spdbooks.org

New Issues Poetry & Prose
Fax P.O. to (269) 387-2562
www.wmich.edu/newissues

24-hour availability on Amazon.com

Examination Copies $5.00

Free Desk Copies with Course Adoption

About Anthony Butts:

Anthony Butts is also the author of *Fifth Season*. His work appears on *Our Souls have Grown Deep like the Rivers: Black Poets Read their Work*; in *Giant Steps: The New Generation of African American Writers*; and in *American Poetry: The Next Generation*. He is a native of Detroit and is a graduate of Wayne State University and the University of Missouri-Columbia. He is a member of the creative writing faculty at Carnegie Mellon University in Pittsburgh, Pennsylvania.

For information about *Little Low Heaven*, contact New Issues Press, 269-387-8185, or see attached information sheet. On the web: www.wmich.edu/newissues

Little Low Heaven

Anthony Butts

New Issues Poetry & Prose

A Green Rose Book

New Issues Poetry & Prose
The College of Arts and Sciences
Western Michigan University
Kalamazoo, Michigan 49008

An Inland Seas Poetry Book

 Inland Seas poetry books are supported by a grant from
The Michigan Council for Arts and Cultural Affairs.

Copyright © 2003 by Anthony Butts. All rights reserved.
Printed in the United States of America.

First Edition, 2003.

ISBN   1930974264 (paperbound)

Library of Congress Cataloging-in-Publication Data:
Butts, Anthony
Little Low Heaven/Anthony Butts
Library of Congress Control Number: 2002113053

Editors   Herbert Scott
                               Derek Pollard
                               Jonathan Pugh
Art Director   Tricia Hennessy
Designer   Shannon Sovia
Production Manager   Paul Sizer
                               The Design Center, Department of Art
                               College of Fine Arts
                               Western Michigan University

Little Low Heaven

Anthony Butts

New Issues

WESTERN MICHIGAN UNIVERSITY

Also by Anthony Butts

Fifth Season
Evolution

The night is far spent; the day draws near.
Let us cast off deeds of darkness and put
on the armor of light.

—*Romans* 13:12

Contents

Fugitive Love

Ars Poetica

—*Detroit, Michigan*

Broad-ribbed leaves of the calathea plant
trickle water down into the mouth of its pot
as if it's still fighting off competitors in the wild

as kittens scamper past, the knees of their
hind legs bending backwards with inhuman
ease, like teenage boys leaping for rebounds

on playgrounds, their hourglass sleekness
glistening like the shards of forty-ounces
littering the court: sons of southern

autoworkers still unfamiliar with the Michigan
that has taken them in, girls watching
from windows as they care for the children

of older sisters. The act of wanting offers
only the hope of movement, for every target
an aim, lives spent in the in-between,

multitudes coexisting in this particular filament
as if no other were possible—American engines
turning in a summertime traffic jam, white clouds

from factories as if shift whistles sent them forth:
the mind propelled by possibility and promise,
an unbreakable stasis. The person who wanted us

has come and gone several times like a tulip
bulb's inhaled and exhaled lives: desire,
the seed itself, creating. See what others

see in us, that gem which no one owns,
our skin a concept, a bloom of imagination
like one's own yearning unfulfilled—unchecked

as poison ivy, the fumes of its combustion
more dangerous than the vine ignored.
Boys want shots to drop. Girls want

what's through the window, not anything
close by or far afield, just the usual.
Cat-backed Swedish and German automobiles

scoot down the boulevard, someone
else's barbecue cooks across the street.
Desire never lies beyond what's given.

I have hated the second-hand world. Who was
that person divided between the glances of passersby?
Bodies decompose, even in memory—

the hand-in-hand of melted hourglass,
bloody hips of gifted tulips detached
and traveling the earth, until the mind

puts an end to them like breakers
washing out to sea. "Fine neighbors,"
someone will say. "Quiet types,"

because no one really knew them
until the press run. Packing kernels inundate
the universe: far off, coalescence; close in,

vibration and sparking. Upon
each smooth surface, each body,
Picasso portraits, light and dark.

Pilots of Evolution

Yellow Archipelago

Nebraskan towns float on waves of corn,
Stone harbors strewn with dust instead
Of sand. Women are stranded downtown, on islands

Along the interstate, where sanity is
An addiction. Everyone is normal here.
The diesel and the locust rule the land.

Lights pass like Morse Code as freighters
Steam through the night. We evolve from the remnants
Of others, the dream catchers and Mardi Gras

Beads left behind. These women are not
Code breakers, never staying awake
Until the wine-dark dawn. The night contains

No secrets, the men at the bar endlessly
Speaking into their ears like auctioneers.
Small talk might keep them awake through

The four o'clock hour: then the hum the earth makes
The only sound beneath the full moon.
The blue molecules of night soak the lawns

As if they'd fallen from the pages of a girl's
Chemistry book. Someday, boys will shoot
Marbles through circles in the dirt.

There's a hole in the middle of the heartland
Where crows sometimes disappear from the tops
Of cornstalks. They resist the pull of gravity

Again, arcing like bloated freighters over
The spurned waves of the archipelago.

Machines

Outside of town, thousands of frogs chortle
And whistle like the frantic sirens and screams
Of an apocalypse, but only the theaters
Are full. Aliens have invaded the earth

Once again. We are never alone, not even
The man who pulls his wife closer in bed
To keep her silent. Her thoughts are like pigeons that crowd
The sidewalks of city parks. The sun rises

Over a misty lake in a starving artist's
Painting. It's the last thing they agreed upon.
Throughout the town, public art stands
At the ready like unnamable metallic

Creatures awaiting a secret message to strike.
A dumpster bears the spray-painted warning:
HEAVEN OR HELL AWAITS YOU as children twirl
Yo-yos with Copernican precision.

A man whispers how machines control
Us all as he watches the toys churn gears.
Pizza delivery vehicles careen
Around corners like the National Guard

On maneuvers. There's a price for being first.
Morning has returned, the sun between
The slats lacing their arms like rubber straps.
Late-night static on television gives way

To a commercial involving local store owners,
Toddlers and canines at their sides. Families are
Truth. In Hartsburg, children, smelly as goats
Or dogs, run through lawns covered with pumpkins.

All is calm but the festival crowds are days
Away when cars will jam the road through town.
Proclamations will shine like copper doorknobs,
Their closing sentences held together by hinges.

Lake of the Spirits

The boys have just returned from drinking and cow
Tipping in the middle of the night.

The bars have all closed. The girls who wouldn't
Dance with them at first are waiting patiently.

Things of this world can be broken. The boy in the mirror
Wears mirrored sunglasses. He calls

The clear piss in the toilet "The Lake of the Spirits."
The water sparkles like dead ponds where chemicals

Extinguish all life. In the smoky walk-up,
Cats have noticeably hidden themselves

Away in the mountains of clothes in the closet.
Even the smell of sex won't make them forget

About being tossed like bowling balls.
The boy will finger the night and reach inside.

He is certain he owns this dark town.
The life-sized cardboard woman

In a bathing suit holding a six-pack
Of beer. Posters of exotic cars.

Anything can happen when his sunglasses
Are removed. The Technicolor of having a new

Girl. When they danced she said "no" to going
Back with him, tapping his shoulder as he walked

Away. Doubt is the conscience of men. They danced
Without regrets. She watched him close his bedroom

Door on the swimsuit model. The night
Held him close. Things of this world can be broken.

Ferris Wheel

His god lived in movies run backwards,
The reels stilled before his warm hand
Reached the co-star's cheek, as if she
Were going to receive a caress instead

Of a smack. His palm retreated slowly at first,
Speeding up as the film unfurled smoothly
In reverse, the near-impact of a gesture
Pulled back suddenly as if he

Were confident but shy, his hand looping
In mid-air and coming to a halt
Intriguingly behind his thigh. The anger
Disappeared. The camera that followed

Them around had been mistaken. And the actress,
His lone audience among the bruised
Seats of the theater, believed what the new world
Revealed, knowing that her rouged cheek

Couldn't really be hurting now. He smiled
As the wheels spun like communion wafers, knowing
That if God exists He exhales in these moments, His chuckle
Bristling the plush darkness. She was enraged

About something, but very glad to have his comforting.
She must have spent the money missing from her
Purse. And he never slept with another woman
He didn't love. (He was faithful to neither.) That reel,

Played backwards, bore his awkward, naked
Backside jerked high and pushed
Low by his invisible god revealed.
He never would promise to enjoy himself.

Every movie was the same, the denuded
Trees anxiously retrieving their leaves:
Clothed in the garments of the living dead.
Dead bodies were resurrected and walked

The earth as if the neutron bomb hadn't
Left their simmered flesh intact. The actress
Was nearly horrified at the sight of the saved
World; he loved warfare. But any

Young man who'd gone to war must
Come home stronger, must be
Reborn knowing that words are greater
Arms: the lengthy spokes of Ferris

Wheels rushing in their double-negative circuits
Forward (but those two remained with his god
Illuminated in the dark: the actor-
Turned-director splicing the celluloid

As if that were the only filming of
The Death of God). In an act of faith, larger
Reels spin forward with vocal children
And adults whirling. Rides are scary

But manageable, as they dent the air
With the concussions of their bursting voices.
The wheel awaits each neophyte
Like the ocular body of Christ held high.

Photograph

Streetlamps capped with miters
Reflect from windows around the alcove,
Hum with the expectation of sunset;

Ashes of leaves trace the wind like incense
Or the secrets of lovers betrayed. A light bulb
Glows in the beveled mirror where a man's

Face should be as he removes the letters
Of a former lover from his bureau,
Its handles like bronzed nipples.

Separation illuminates the flesh. Devotion
Blurs boundaries, mixes metaphors until
The mood replaces us, the blue visage

Of a chapel chiming hours by the alcove,
Its dentils lining the underside of the roof,
Its steeple fending the trees for light above
A couple speaking quietly in the shadow.

The Lover of Birds

Silver Nitrate

Bedsheets shield the outside world,
the screened sun yearning
to filter through. Passersby seem
ghostly negatives in cold intervals
of intimacy, my skin like black ice forming
beneath the chill of her palms' slippage.
She would not cage her birds.
They came willingly and she forgave them
their inclination towards flight,
as she forgave me. The sky was patched.
When cardinals stained the yard like blood
she would whistle, a lover in waiting.
We would tend to the birds descending
like palms. The seed I scattered
kept them, sustaining balance,
as she slipped behind the screen door.
I am a silhouette on a park bench,
hands dispersing in every direction, my body
trembling, a nest of wings, or a grainy photo forming.

Transmissions

Hailstones fall from the clear half
of a Michigan sky, tall pewter clouds
billowing forth umbrellas
turned inside-out like radio telescopes
to Mars. No one listens.
I am unable to speak.
The night's revelations incomplete
except for kisses withheld.
My sisters in their sleep unaware
of the proper translation of *reticence.*

Are my eyes the only sign of absence
on the glacial plateau of thrown sheets?
I feel abandoned here, my body as austere
as ice, her fingers like the beaks of penguins,
an afterimage of lightning fleshing out
the darkness of startled secrets
like illuminations of a sacred text.

Reconnaissance

Balls of sweet gum, the buds
of magnolias gutted, seedlings camouflaged
in green. Songbirds direct coded verses
towards the sky as if to signal
reconnaissance is no longer necessary.

She reaches her hands down to me.
The ceiling clouds, seagulls cruise inland,
brighter bodies flashing between storms
like pure light. She says how gulls
are drawn to pilings as if they are poised
to speak but remain silent.

A pale sun drones through the city,
indiscriminate red buds bursting, redwing
blackbirds buzzing the schoolyard bullies.
Instinct is action practiced to a fault,
victim pummeling victim until the sheer need
to survive becomes the framework for wings.

An Asian woman shields her head as she walks
to a school building in this season of dread,
couples holding hands for the first time in months,
an entire year boxed away like unwanted Christmas gifts or anger.

Mist soaks the reeds of a pond,
ducks and geese murmuring in their sleep
before a sunrise that will burn it all off.

The Robin's Egg

In my hand, a hazy blue robin's egg
like the earth as seen from orbit,
or God's eye peering down in judgment,

but no one is here in the overcast noon
of April, the turf thick as a putting green
from eons of peat sown by glaciers

that gouged the Great Lakes into being.
I won't discuss it with her, shut
in her house as if tracking the evolution

of isolated species. I don't want to study
the shriveled chick lurking within,
its heart the only pulsing, a dark cosmos

awaiting the light of Creation. Apple blossoms
open their gateways to heaven. Tissue flowers
decorate the side panels of Cadillacs, black steel glistening

like moist soil, the newlyweds enclosed within.
Whirlybirds descend from maples like husks
from the Hall of Souls, that first loss.

The Shadowbox

No photographs of me hang
in my parents' shadowbox,
infants and graduates in their
various caps, the mirror ringed
with siblings. I will never
marry. I won't be kissed
or drink my mother's milk.
It's clouded. A black bird went out,
a white one came back. This is
a house of aliens, my real mother alone
in her home with my pictures, the blades
of her fan turning behind wire guards
curved like sperm swimming,
my history invisible. She's drinking again
in the pastel half-light of dusk layered
like the pink and purple sand in a clear
bottle, her coleuses lined up
like aunts before the nursery window
of the child one will take.

Vespers

Rose Window

The choir flings its voices over the balcony,
the kneeling pews in rectangular furrows
below. None are alike. The basses
hollow out around the midsection

like carp. The pearls of the altos hang
in motherly parabolas like visible outlines
of milk overflowing. A tenor shivers
in the stratospheric notes of sopranos,

light glancing off the wedges of their precise faces
like eyes too shy to encounter them directly.
A rose window hovers behind
like an iris that might drop tears

the size of hymnals. The tenor
disappears into the mountain
air. Only the body of his voice remains.
He wanders through the oaken pews

as a holy spirit until he comes face to face
with the sheer pool of a woman rippling,
her sanctified body evaporating
into the rosy light where the voices are waiting.

Spring Romance

Frail branches extend from pale trees,
their trunks the width of pelvic bones. Ashes
sway in the decaying evidence of
March, the soil moist in the new-found

absence of snow, bacteria reproducing
like lovers roiling in the black peat.
The smell of pine no longer fills the hollow
midsection of winter, the newborn

spring a faint haze of green. He can
see his reflection in a pool of tarnished
liquid, an ice mound melting near
its center. It isn't him. The water lies.

Instead of eyelashes, he sees the needles
of a hawthorn; instead of hair, leaves and the petals
of flowers. He witnesses his own funeral
as he kneels on the ground.

A bony woman watches from the trunks
behind him, this man who is squat like a hawthorn
yet large as an evergreen—his hair
ossifying into a garment of needles.

The Silk Gardens

He walks past a corner home where canaries
beat their yellow tail feathers, one
over the other's, behind the pear-green
panes. The historic district is his favorite

path for evening hikes, the brim of a black
fedora flipped down over his brow,
the moist air sweetened by the scent
of distant skunk, pin-oak leaves

blowing in the dusky breeze. A man
sits in his bay window stitching swatches
into a shantung evening gown,
into the terrain of his wife—asleep

in her daybed—his chestnut knuckles
like the joints of a spider crawling across the sheer
fronds of palm trees. The fluorescent
tubes of a college library glow

like toy worms, their parallel skins
hanging in rows of dizzying pairs, the silken
light falling through the musty air, their bodies
coupling firmly outside this night.

In Fear of Winter

The creatures seem to disappear as snow
falls in flakes the size of buttons, the gray
noon fastened down like a sofa cushion,
the muffled air laboring to breathe.

The limbs of trees flash their charcoal
lightning overhead, their green leaves
withheld like winter's thunder, branches
bobbing wrists in a violin section.

A man sits on a park bench, allowing
the snow to hem his shoulders.
Others remain in the still cocoons
of their living rooms like caterpillars snoozing.

The concert hall reveals an orchestra practicing,
the white cuffs of shirts poking like prairie dogs
out of the black cylinders of sleeves.

The violinists carve their strings
as a slender Ukrainian pianist
deftly kills each previous chord,
damning the keys with her long white fingers.

Empty Christmas Boxes

The girls in their red and blue velour
dresses spin into their seats after
intermission, their parents having taken
many of them to *The Nutcracker*

even before kindergarten. On stage,
ballerinas twirl like the frail dust
devils in the right-angle cradles
of junior high school brick buildings.

In winter, grains of snow replace the dust
to spin like stones in the tumbler of the gift
he'd always wanted, a toy that promised to turn
rocks into gems. He watches the beveled snow

gleaming like the eyes of carousel
horses rising and falling as they circle.
A blue spruce stands next to his window,
empty Christmas boxes beneath.

Like the tree itself, the presents are ornamental.
Ornate fish await feeding time
beneath the eerie florescence, their scales like crushed
velvet, their fins like little girls' scarves.

Invocation to Mary of Michigan

Sleet falls like shards from a broken mirror,
her face hidden between the crystals.
Lady of the Snow, it's cold
but they will be alone no longer.

A man's face fashions a stern mold
from the fog. Pellets drop like stars through the night,
roads of shining galaxies coalescing
beneath his boots. Her icy coat stands

firm against the wind, her green leggings
sprouting beneath a rose-colored skirt.
Lady of the Snow, it's cold
but they will be alone no longer.

Each crystal contains a miniature
October, the colors garlanding a parish
within. She witnesses the universe collapsing,
at the mercy of gravity, each pellet a gem,

a sun setting. She feels the warmth of their orbits
skimming her face, in each sphere a man stranded.
Lady of the Snow, it's cold
but they will be alone no longer.

Dry Seed

Fornication

I have walked without a shadow,
the sun stalled at noon for years,
all traces of memory clipped from me
as if they were bits of paper, origami animals
mired in the dark pool my body casts
in dreams, in the only shadow that remains.

Down a street lined with hawthorns,
through clouds of their fumes,
spring bears her flowers like a lover,
petals buoyed on air, the scent
as thick as water. I am not drowning,
not spiraling out of the unwanted embrace
of a whirlpool or waterspout whose currents
might never release me from his arms
washing over me: a small ship
tossed by the large sea, my shadow now
floating alone, the body submerged.

He was the god of forlorn rivers,
of heavy water lurking in its bed,
crashing against the boundaries
of any bank or bow. In the fumes of trees,
in that invisible fog spilling over the banks
of narrow streams, my shadow was snagged
on the pike of a hawthorn branch, caught
like cotton candy streaming its pink flesh
through midnight leaves.

                    In the androgynous light
of an eclipse of the sun I can feel the tug;
my shadow drags behind in the solitary light.
The noonday sun hangs it from a tree, the scent
of hawthorns flowing as if from the delta
of an ordinary woman.

Butterflies

My mouth is swollen with false viruses,
a river of antennae pushing against the banks

of my body, his unmistakable voice
more contagious than any real disease.

I am a plum grown round the place
where my seed should've been, a moist womb

sustained by threats and sex. The world
shimmers with the dual light of fluid worlds,

every object both animate and inert,
the confident voice of a woman crawling

like a caterpillar out of its cocoon to discover
grown wings. Her voice hovers

just beyond the railing, just out of view,
having sailed through the room

awakening every object that passed beneath
its wings. My throat undulates like a cocoon,

arms and legs moving in waves beneath my skin,
an ocean of sex, a meditation on the patterns

of the present and the past washing over me.
The world is made of water and air, an orgasm

of elemental desires, even the railing and the walls
rippling in half-time to the rhythm of her voice,

to the rhythm of my body shedding like a snake.
Words alone will not remake the world, a chimera

of nouns and verbs sloughed off with my skin
in a monstrous pile of tattoos. During sex

a caterpillar writhes in my throat, yearning
to transform itself. I can say what he did

to a three-year-old child if I say it with my body,
lighter than liquid air, a shimmering haven

of double images where my thoughts become wings
that will carry me to the voice beyond this room.

Cyclones

The apocalypse did not come as was foretold
because he only claimed to be Jesus,
laying his hands firmly on my head
in the same unsteady motion
that I was to later see in nature.

I was a marigold and he was a bee
hovering indecisively over me, shifting
from left to right, in his triangulation
of desire, in the living science of math,
as hot and cold as the air of spring.

God is the pea-green dome above the rain,
his voice a fluctuating command for me
to be first hot then cold then hot again
in a perfect dance to copy the quick and fickle
repetition that forced me to remain awake.

But I believed my petals were as much a part
of that storm as he himself, my body
organized around his desire, hot and cold winds
cycling until I became a rapid swirl of both,
and older than the land that I was standing on.

My body was no longer mine, eyes deeper than world
without end, a bottomless shaft of wind churning
around a center without form, bits and pieces
of landscape torn, reconstituted
as I roamed, like him, with godlike will.

His boredom equaled anger, the equation that inspires
excitement, my body shedding a mass of heavy water
lobbed like lodestones through the air, every splinter
a javelin, every fleck in my eyes a section of wooden
windmills, turning like swords of Eden.

Spellbound

My body is the landscape of conversations,
with brigands wandering through the new earth
beneath this sycamore, my skin shedding a spiral
of double meanings, in the husks of my words
descending like dry seed through the air.

There was a time when I thought that my body
was only the landscape of the earth—until a lover took me
to the center of the lake to make me swim for the first time,
and I knew that I had seen the shore from there
before, when I needed to float and not to sink.

I was innocent, my arms and legs flailing against
the first waves that restrained me, my words
like stones lobbed back to shore
in a siege of misunderstanding, in the metaphor
that would signal my rebirth like a comet passing.

I was reborn to live in the image
he had of me, a conjurer, a living shadow
that cast its spell upon him like the moon does
during an eclipse of the sun, the world drowned
in the light of night and day.

All the animals of the earth listened to me,
disturbed by a sudden sense of night, responding
to the charmed voices of my human companions calling
like cardinals to each other as if I were not present,
as if my voice were not responsible for leading them.

Because of him I learned not only to map the landscape
of conversations but to quicken them, my every word
birthing twin connotations until I was surrounded
by a family of gypsies who would never reveal the road
that led back to the lake where I was safely floating.

Sunset

The memory of him still pricking,
striking lights behind my lids,
the world created of images
repeated in the hallowed eyes
of gods. My veins were filled with viruses

that guided false diseases through me
as a dense, unseen array that hazed my organs:
the northern lights encircling pine trees.
A blizzard brought him back to me
in the season where I took refuge.

Did he feel lights like stripped-down
collapsars spinning towards decay? He crawled up
the sloped steps towards those lights. I wondered
if the gods he showed me welcomed his return.
Parts of him were gangrenous,

or half asleep, or drugged
in the kind of sleep I'd always wanted.
I had to please those gods who placed
themselves in him, the pulsing lights
of day repeated in migraines

that flickered even in darkness.
I closed myself
from the light inside. But God has strewn
the dusk in arcing sunsets, one sphere
after another. I could not clear *that* canvas,

a hemisphere of suns spackling the sky,
until I slept beneath the torn but radiant sheet
of my desire, the sky ripped black and fringed
by a white as pure as paper, the unobtrusive God
peering down from the periphery.

Skin

In this world, shadows do not speak to us.
But when I write in shadows they call out
to me. I feel guilt for talking back,
  which should prove my humanity.

They move. The wings
of monarch butterflies flitter down into fields
like leaves in autumn. Wings are shadows
    in my throat and they speak with me.
    They write their names on my skin
    as fervently as my brother did.

I have been a rapid angel since ending his game:
my awkward insides weren't really all mine. I would
disappear when he carved his name on my skin.
    He showed me I was just one word
    and I was made to never speak of it.

He told a lie to cover me up; I would never own
a unique body of cells. I'm dark and unseen
unlike the Christmas boxes
    in my dreams with their fervent stripes
    of pink and white skin. He was so happy
    about my insides that he would write
on me; and his name was silence.

The world of desire is too strong
for my body, but I can no longer sing of it
backwards, the falsetto scales
    of troubled notes; I was upside-down for him,
    disappearing. I feel him ascending now
    out of my body unlike some finger
that he would slip in; his name passes up
and away through trails in my skin.
True memories are fires within.
    New hair curls his name backwards.
    And I will flitter now, as I couldn't before;

lives are born and born again.
I have been a rapid angel since falling
    to earth; this paper, this skin, is mine.

Fugitive Love

Poem to be Hummed

I am standing before a gathering of those
whose eyes are a gentle sea barely visible, all of us viewing
something near the poetry that isn't us,
nor the poet as he was then, nor even some fellow rowing,
keenly aware of his small presence:
a void so familiar we dare not fear it
or ask why we don't recall it in other moments.

Where do visions go? To the same
sanctuary as jazz artists at the completion
of a set—that magical green room we've only dreamt of?
Are we not something other than what we are?
The slender librarian in a sheer flowered dress,
the canary-yellow convertible rolling by?
Visions of beauty survive in the preserve
for what we no longer keep.

Most of us know the green room
was never meant for us but for the mythological
jazz man with all his faults, unable to switch off
whatever it is within us that we could never
switch on, our emotions like acute angles—
more a fear of consumption by mouths
than the opposing pull of what we see before us:
that we seek out the myths that we believe in,
an endless space having enveloped us long ago.

Fugit Amor

—*Rodin Museum, Paris (Auguste Rodin, 1887)*

The empty space within the sculpture of man and woman
renders its shape: bronze backs—opposing each other—arched
like symbols for yin and yang, the bodies somber

as trees at dusk, leaves sooty before the disembarking blue.
Black like letters upon the page, night attempts to obscure
what we ourselves cannot—our hollow bodies, lips
opening and closing like those of bawdy carnival mannequins.

Fugitive love; still lives; carpenter ants; confessionals;
progressing undisturbed: unpicked apples black in the orchard,
new lovers engaged in the dark profile of desire unachieved:

their bent coils of esophagi, the limitations of vertebrae and longing.
The vulnerable are vessels of wisdom, children who know
before the filing of papers: nothing in the house can obscure
its presence. It inhabits even the inner walls of their eyelids

until they believe it's gone, the freedom of invisibility.

The Model

From this wheelchair drawn across paper,
across blameless desire; in the erasure of distance,
in the tumult when we come too close, I feel the sky
cloud the ground in Victorian green, in needy rain
and hail. From their vantage, the students map
the parallax of loss—pencils scratching
in arcs like bees that take aim on the marigolds
in my yard. Approximations of the sun,
a world without objects. The color creeps
quietly out of my skin, out of the minds
of women who ink children into their dreams.

Draw my skin in crosshatch silence; make a flesh
of shadow, of the template of seduction when lovers
stand this close—of the standard chill of autumn
brought on by our birthing. I am a small someone
and the trees are made of broccoli, crisp and cool
as the fingers of a woman snatching
marigolds from sleep, or icicles dropping
mad fat tears when seen at a distance. Words
spill from graphite, the soft flesh masking the silence,
the hard wood cradling the loss.

The Nut Gatherers

—*Detroit Institute of Arts*
(William Adolphe Bouguereau, 1882)

When viewed aslant, the painting
reveals the truer glance of the fairer girl—

not quite in the direction of her modest partner
surprised beneath track lights gathering

hulls before patrons and docents
and the guards who keep watch over

the one man angling nearer the horizon
of the frame, the landscape thinning

out of existence before he meets her gaze:
as close as he's ever come to the act of creation.

Someone's wife wanders amidst blown glass—
the mouths blossoming from small sacs

lying flat along the table, the dark throats
bottomless as if emphasizing the lack of roses,

chimerical bodies frozen in mid-scream, light
cast in the visible spectra of voices

like the unspoken shorthand of couples
arguing—her body almost detectable

within the glare as pure light or as
the definition of words left unsaid in the night.

A schoolgirl watches the man before *The Nut Gatherers*
swaying near the new land's edge, a room

within a room, amongst the gallery's traffic,
which no one enters, a class passing through

indistinguishable from the rest as other doors
open and shut before her. Perhaps she knows what the girl

in the painting knows, that our eyes negate
our wishes as walls assume themselves around us,

inexplicably keeping us warm in winter,
cool in summer, until we finally give in—

the wife opening a door with her eyes,
herself unprepared for what she cannot want.

What's Not Given

Sitting on the coffeehouse patio
she reads the newspaper,
its classifieds attesting to lovers
of sunsets as no one notices
the break in the clouds, brownstones
and maples dripping with diminishing
light, her husband stirring his coffee
as other men sip and stroll through
sweet ragweed: their most emotional
season. Another train traverses
the overpass painted in pseudo
Indian designs, trapezoidal coal cars
and tubular oil tankers clanking
over rails that meet only
in the distance like dreams
realized or words rehearsing
the essence of ideas, or beauty
masquerading as truth.
The mocha stain on the table,
the filmy window of the café,
humid heat rising off pavement
as the sun breaks free in tremors
of cirrus across the sky—
we must have faith in what's not given—
extrapolations of the sensory world,
her own reflection, the dark spaces
fringed by order: not the paper,
nor the sunset, nor the man and his coffee, but
her green sunglasses restraining the pink sky,
her hand sweeping back loose hair once again.
She will not notice those flecked irises staring back
from the insides of her sunglasses like lights meeting
as two trains assemble through the dark
on the one perfect track between them.

Blue Periods

Blackbirds on bare branches,
like forbidden fruit, upside-down
drop towards the pre-dawn clouds.

Only her hair and eyes and lips
are visible, a tricolor standard
behind the mist, in horizontals

of black, lapis and ruby—her skin
a worn patina. We can gauge
only what has left us behind, the sediment

of time collected in linen until sleep
becomes a shore for primordial seas,
windows hovering outside, silent measures

in musical scores above morning traffic.
Women stroll down Brown Street,
the brown roots of their blonde hair

hanging on like spines of anemone,
their faces opaque in comparison.
Men drift in and out of the shoddy slate houses,

the refuge of melancholy artists
standing pale before wet canvases.

The End of All

I no longer believe in prophesy, the mimetic universe giving
a dope fiend just what he needs, his mirror lenses confounding
me with my own coherence; or other concepts as troubling as desire:
the waitress who fingers her tips, her boyfriend who does not resemble me.
They found each other via the internet as "Venus" and "Mars"

flickering eerily as fireflies on the screens of salvaged monitors,
both laughing and laughed at, rhythms of a jazz quintet
leaping like separate selves of Athena repeatedly born.

Rembrandt could've painted his self-portrait enough times
to overrun the earth, each unique yet similar, grids of the individual
psyche gazing upon what could never be: a world deferred by our dreaming.

It may take weeks of writing a poem in which the perfect
woman should've appeared before the poet figures
that "asphodel" is a word worth singing repeatedly.

I am surrounded by fields of electrical snow obscuring
favorite shows of lost decades—as if I were vibrant
as words or other created forms: straw stuffed up
the skirt of an unknown woman who may have only once
donated to the Goodwill, on the day before leaving Oklahoma for Reno.

Yellow candles on a windowsill bear witness to the smoky hue
of the harvest moon illuminating the figure of a model
in a skin magazine, her body smoother than that of her living counterpart,
but drabber than the words which recreate them both, like love notes
reread even after the skittish breakup, *that* self more real than this one.

In spite of us, the ceaseless present pushes forward, those
trapped in past worlds forever distanced from those trapped here,
our only faith the nexus of remembrance and conception: neither
living nor dead, nor love song nor elegy—through the haze of excess
the only wish: that there will never be more worlds like these.

To the Woman Who Does Not Exist

1.
White pigeons in winter beneath eaves,
behind icicles, wings imperceptible
except for their flapping, echoes
of their bodies trailing in intervals.
Sound is more methodical than time.
His singing the link between disparate items.
The clock ticks obscurity into existence
as a dark dawn approaches for the man
who does not exist to witness.

Headstones up the hill, hopeful
and ruminative, their marbled surfaces
aglint in the winter fog, a hall
of mirrors multiplying; he walks
unnoticed. The bone end of his fingertip
taps out the bent steel of language
on a woman's cold stone.

2.
A husband packs a plastic bag with bean sprouts,
their stalks like the skeletal digits of infants
through the dirt of mass graves. His wife tests the bottoms
of zucchini and eggplant as if they were never children—
as if they sought only her touch and not conception.

The dead have desires, the living
needs—the unseen man walking up the aisle
as if he's been noticed, a ravenous void passing.

3.
He knows that he cannot really see himself
in the eyes of a woman shopping for produce;
it's the rolling apples which draw her attention
to the place where someone may have been.
The mirrors hold a collection of dots
which might be the air, something in it passing

like a thought, or a vampire of light.
She does not see any of this,
but is drawn to wisps of air disturbed
as if blown through her perfect hair.
It never fades, this sense
that we are perpetually alone.
The hairs on his neck stand on end.
The mirrors whisper their bodies into being, into time.

In the Museum of Language

1.
Through the distance transfixed in silence,
like bound pages yellowing upon shelves,
we seem to gather dust, residue of sleep
from eyes that won't revive another pale wife
beneath a blue parasol, or even review
the horizontal gestures of emotion diffused,
our bodies caught in the unfamiliar present,
like Osiris in mid-stride, or Narcissus gazing
into the nature of his being. Art dismisses life.
A Victorian woman sits calmly, patterns
springing up around her in a language
perhaps the gladioli understand, our otherness
made inconceivable yet holy as we turn away,
inchoate and mute, towards new-found lands
which may refuse to take us in—until nowhere
becomes home, visions of our future,
our mother tongue, revealed to all but ourselves
and the unyielding faces we seek in dreams.

2.
When the world went dark, some of us
gathered in coves, our backs against granite.
The progression of knowledge had ceased.
No one ventured forth in silence to learn language.
Few could remember the light that would bookend
darkness. We were at rest in a place
where everything had always been possible.
We knew we could never go back.
Not the man with fresh cigarette burns
beneath his woolen clothes like notes
from lovers newly discovered,
nor the thin woman hugging herself,
believing only God could love her,
her blouse like a sail headed for distant territories
where the natives are fierce yet capable of love.
We huddled together, wanting meaning
beyond language or human will.

3.
From inside our bodies a gangplank lowers
onto the shore of a new continent
that will come to own us no more
than the last nor haunt us any less.
Yet with every incarnation:
the alien within us relinquished.

Acknowledgments

Grateful acknowledgement is made to the editors and publishers of the following publications in which these poems first appeared, sometimes in previous versions, and to the Ohio Arts Council for an Individual Artist Grant, which allowed me the time and space for the completion of this book:

Callaloo: "Machines," "What's Not Given," "Yellow Archipelago"

The Canary River Review: "Reconnaissance," "Sunset"

Cimarron Review: "To the Woman Who Does Not Exist," "Butterflies"

Crab Orchard Review: "Ferris Wheel"

Fourteen Hills: The SFSU Review: "Silver Nitrate"

Literature and Belief: "Invocation to Mary of Michigan"

Meridian: "Lake of the Spirits"

the minnesota review: "Cyclones," "Spellbound"

New Letters: "Spring Romance"

Pleiades: "In Fear of Winter" (published as "The Loudest Sound")

Prairie Schooner: "The Model"

Whiskey Island Magazine: "Blue Periods"

"Skin" appeared in *American Poetry: The Next Generation,* Carnegie Mellon University Press

"Machines" and "In Fear of Winter" (published as "The Loudest Sound") appeared in *Giant Steps: The New Generation of African American Writers,* Harper Perennial

"Yellow Archipelago" appeared in *New Poems from the Third Coast,* Wayne State University Press

Many thanks to Sherod Santos, Lynne McMahon, and Ellie Ragland for their support in the completion of most of the poems presented here. Special thanks to Herbert Scott.

photo by Mat Bulvony

Anthony Butts is also the author of *Fifth Season*. His work appears
on *Our Souls Have Grown Deep Like the Rivers: Black Poets Read
Their Work;* in *Giant Steps: The New Generation of African American
Writers;* and in *American Poetry: The Next Generation.* A Detroit
native, he is a graduate of Wayne State University and the University
of Missouri-Columbia, and a member of the creative writing faculty
at Carnegie Mellon University in Pittsburgh, Pennsylvania.

New Issues Poetry & Prose

Editor, Herbert Scott

Vito Aiuto, *Self-Portrait as Jerry Quarry*
James Armstrong, *Monument In A Summer Hat*
Claire Bateman, *Clumsy*
Michael Burkard, *Pennsylvania Collection Agency*
Christopher Bursk, *Ovid at Fifteen*
Anthony Butts, Fifth Season
Anthony Butts, *Little Low Heaven*
Kevin Cantwell, *Something Black in the Green Part of Your Eye*
Gladys Cardiff, *A Bare Unpainted Table*
Kevin Clark, *In the Evening of No Warning*
Jim Daniels, *Night with Drive-By Shooting Stars*
Joseph Featherstone, *Brace's Cove*
Lisa Fishman, *The Deep Heart's Core Is a Suitcase*
Robert Grunst, *The Smallest Bird in North America*
Paul Guest, *The Resurrection of the Body and the Ruin of the World*
Robert Haight, *Emergences and Spinner Falls*
Mark Halperin, *Time as Distance*
Myronn Hardy, *Approaching the Center*
Edward Haworth Hoeppner, *Rain Through High Windows*
Cynthia Hogue, *Flux*
Janet Kauffman, *Rot* (fiction)
Josie Kearns, *New Numbers*
Maurice Kilwein Guevara, *Autobiography of So-and-so: Poems in Prose*
Ruth Ellen Kocher, *When the Moon Knows You're Wandering*
Steve Langan, *Freezing*
Lance Larsen, *Erasable Walls*
David Dodd Lee, *Downsides of Fish Culture*
Deanne Lundin, *The Ginseng Hunter's Notebook*
Joy Manesiotis, *They Sing to Her Bones*
Sarah Mangold, *Household Mechanics*
David Marlatt, *A Hog Slaughtering Woman*
Gretchen Mattox, *Goodnight Architecture*
Paula McLain, *Less of Her*
Sarah Messer, *Bandit Letters*
Malena Mörling, *Ocean Avenue*
Julie Moulds, *The Woman with a Cubed Head*
Gerald Murnane, *The Plains* (fiction)
Marsha de la O, *Black Hope*
C. Mikal Oness, *Water Becomes Bone*
Elizabeth Powell, *The Republic of Self*
Margaret Rabb, *Granite Dives*
Rebecca Reynolds, *Daughter of the Hangnail; The Bovine Two-Step*